contents

Before you start

about this book

Have fun with musical sounds in this book. Each instrument is simple to make, using easy-to-find materials. Use your imagination to experiment with different sounds and rhythms. Design and decorate your own twisting drum, tambourine, rhythm sticks and many more exciting instruments. Once you have tried out the projects in this book, enjoy making more ideas of your own.

Tools and materials

You will need paints and a paintbrush for most projects. Gouache paints are the best, because they are thick, dry fast and cover well.

Once the paint is *completely* dry, add a coat of clear varnish (you can use PVA glue). This will give the instruments a shiny, long-lasting finish.

Use a different paintbrush for varnishing. You will also need scissors, glue and a ruler for many of the projects. All the tools and materials you will need are listed at the start of each project.

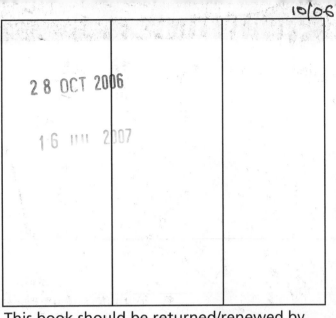

10/06

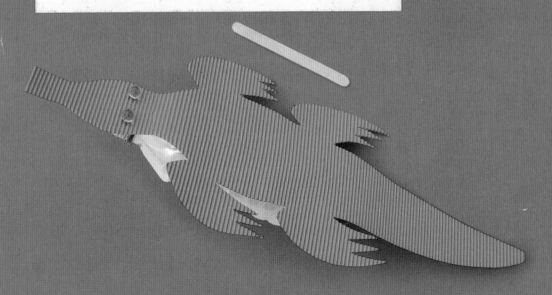

W
FRANKLIN WATTS
LONDON•SYDNEY

This edition published in 2006 by
Franklin Watts
338 Euston Road
London NW1 3BH

Franklin Watts Australia
Hachette Children's Books
Level 17/207 Kent Street
Sydney NSW 2000

Originally published by
Casterman, Belgium
Original edition © Casterman 1998
English edition © Franklin Watts 2006

Text and illustrations: Brigitte van de Wouwer
Photography: Daniel Lippert
Design: Dominique Mazy
Translation: Ruth Thomson

ISBN-10: 0 7496 6907 1
ISBN-13: 978 0 7496 6907 2

A CIP catalogue record for this book is
available from the British Library.

Dewey Classification: 784.1923'

Printed in China

Quick and easy ideas

1 Cut off the neck of a balloon and blow through it. Pull the end longer and longer to make the sound higher and higher.

2 Make maracas by gluing two plastic yogurt pots together with rice grains inside.

3 Whistle across a pen lid to imitate bird song.

4 Make castanets. Thread elastic through large, slightly concave buttons, making loops for your index finger and thumb.

5 Fit one plastic pot with corrugated sides into another. Hold the bottom pot and swivel the top one to make a rattling sound.

6 Thread metallic buttons on to some string. Shake them with a rhythmical beat.

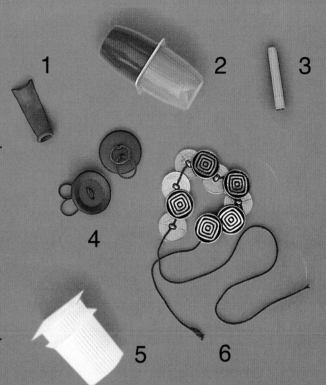

Learning logos

The activities in the book provide practice in different skills, identified by the logos below.

An activity practising
imagination and creativity

An activity practising
fine motor control

An activity practising
spatial skills

Bell

clay flowerpot ● gouache paints ● paintbrush ● beads
PVA glue or varnish ● large button
string ● wool or raffia

1 Paint a face on a large bead. Paint a dress and arms on the flowerpot. When the paint is dry, varnish both of them.

2 Knot one end of some string. Thread on a small bead.

3 Make a knot higher up and thread on another bead for the clanger. Make a third knot even higher up. Thread on a large bead, the pot and the head. Make sure the clanger hits the pot.

Make a plait of wool or raffia, knotting both ends. Thread the string though the middle of the plait, so that it sits on the top of the head. Finally, thread on the button as a hat.

HOW TO PLAY THE BELL

Hold the string above the girl's head in one hand. Pull the string with the bead to clang the bell.

Rhythm sticks

two rounded wooden sticks ● gouache paints
paintbrush ● PVA glue or varnish

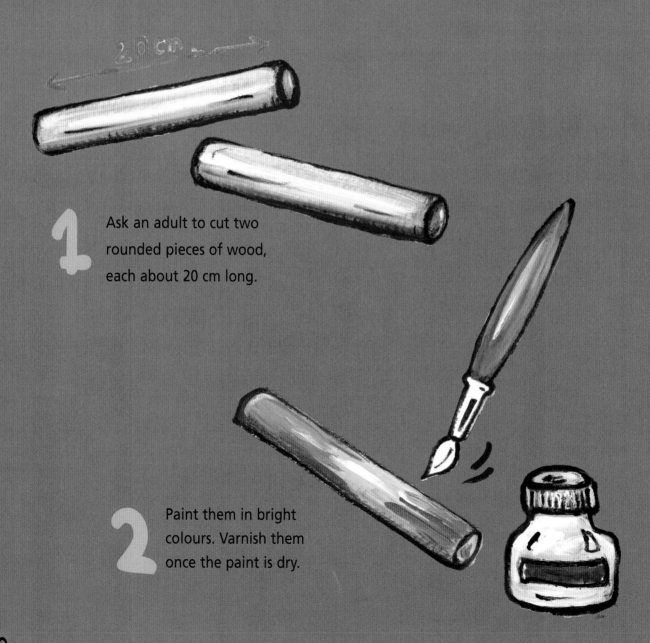

1 Ask an adult to cut two rounded pieces of wood, each about 20 cm long.

2 Paint them in bright colours. Varnish them once the paint is dry.

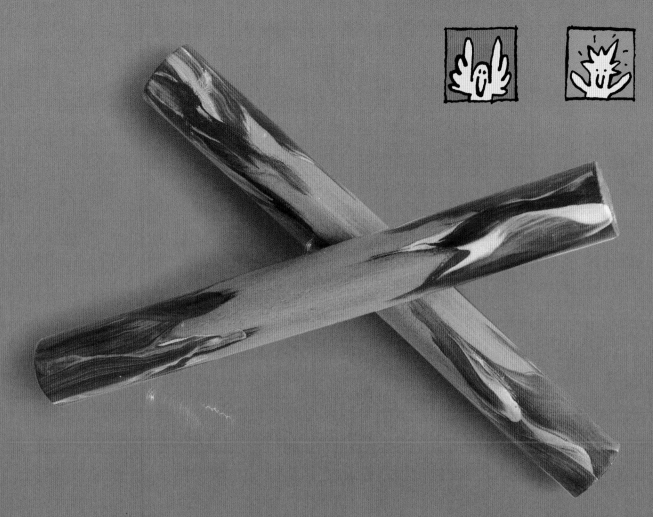

HOW TO PLAY RHYTHM STICKS

Hold one stick loosely across your left hand. Curve your palm and bend all your fingers to create a little sound chamber. Use the other stick as a beater.

Twisting drum

empty cheese box with lid ● wooden stick or pencil
scissors ● two beads ● string ● masking tape
gouache paints ● paintbrush ● PVA glue or varnish

1 Cut a small opening in the side of the cheese box and its lid. The cuts should be big enough for a stick or pencil to fit through.

2 Cut two pieces of string, each about 5 cm long and knot one end. Thread a bead on to each one.

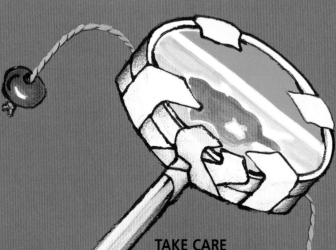

TAKE CARE
When you fix the strings in place, make sure the beads hit the middle of the box.

3 Close the box, fitting in the stick as a handle and the beaded strings on either side as beaters. Tape them all in place.

Paint a funny face on the drum. Varnish it when the paint is completely dry.

HOW TO PLAY THE DRUM
Roll the handle quickly to and fro between your hands to get a fast, regular beat.

13

Harp

wooden coat hanger ● long rubber bands ● hammer
two nails ● empty tin can (without a sharp rim)
gouache paints ● paintbrush ● PVA glue or varnish
ice-lolly stick or spatula

1 Paint and varnish the tin can and hanger. Ask an adult to bang in a nail at either end of the hanger.

2 Stretch a few rubber bands between the nails. Fit the tin can between the hanger and the rubber bands.

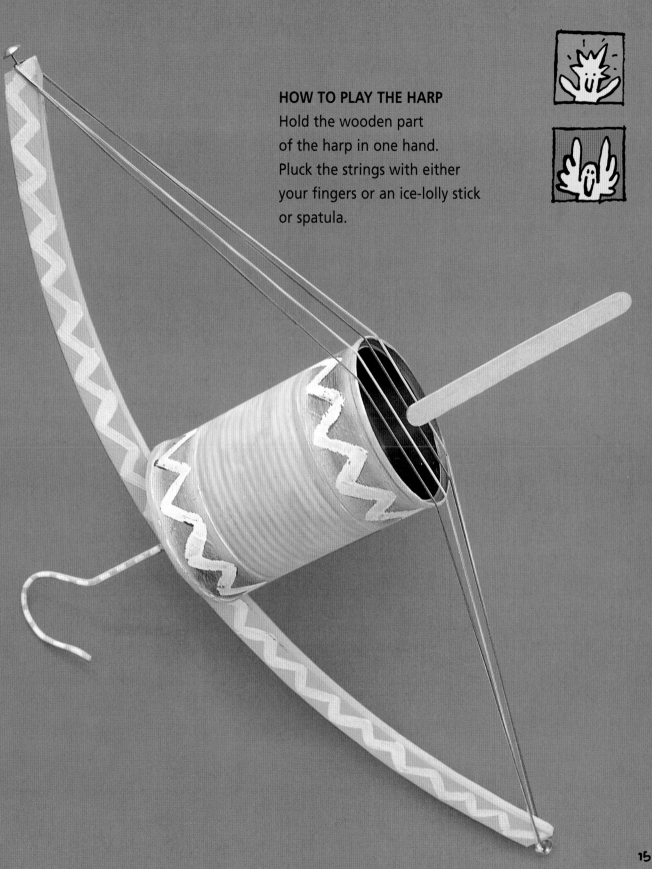

HOW TO PLAY THE HARP

Hold the wooden part
of the harp in one hand.
Pluck the strings with either
your fingers or an ice-lolly stick
or spatula.

Tambourine

empty cardboard roll of sticky tape ● scissors ● paintbrush
gouache paints ● two balloons ● glue ● thin, bendy wire
wooden stick ● metal buttons

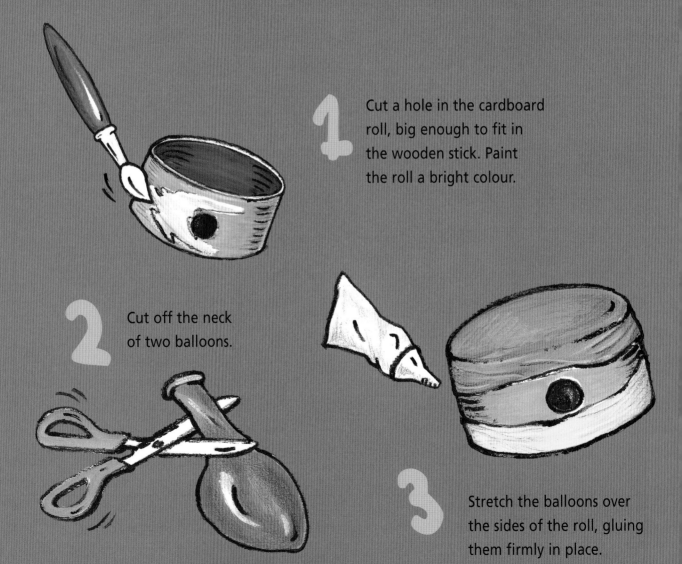

1 Cut a hole in the cardboard roll, big enough to fit in the wooden stick. Paint the roll a bright colour.

2 Cut off the neck of two balloons.

3 Stretch the balloons over the sides of the roll, gluing them firmly in place.

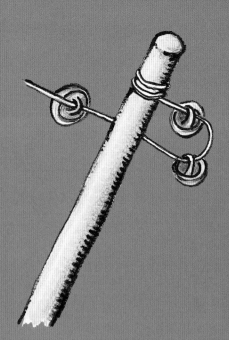

Thread the metal buttons on to a length of wire. Tightly twist one end of the wire to the stick. Loosely twist the rest so the buttons can rattle, then tightly twist the other end around the stick.

HOW TO PLAY THE TAMBOURINE
Hold the tambourine by the handle and shake it. At the same time, hit it with your other hand or a beater.

Shaker

empty matchbox ● ice-lolly stick ● rice grains ● paintbrush
gouache paints ● PVA glue or varnish ● large rubber band

1 Paint the matchbox. Once the paint is completely dry, varnish it.

2 Put a handful of rice grains into the box.

3 Close the box, sliding in the lolly stick. Fix it in place with a rubber band, as shown.

HOW TO PLAY THE SHAKER
Shake the instrument
with short, sharp,
rhythmical strokes.

Tom-tom

large, empty yogurt pot ● paintbrush ● gouache paints
scissors ● PVA glue or varnish ● balloon

2 Paint and varnish it.

1 Wash and dry the yogurt pot. Cut a large hole in its base.

3 Put a line of glue around the top rim.

4 Cut off the neck of the balloon. Stretch the balloon over the top of the pot.

**HOW TO PLAY
THE TOM-TOM**
Use a beater
or your fingers to
beat the tom-tom.

Guitar

empty shoebox ● scissors ● masking tape ● gouache paints
paintbrush ● PVA glue or varnish ● large rubber bands
wooden clothes peg ● ice-lolly stick or wooden spatula

1 Cut out an oval-shaped hole in the centre of the box base.

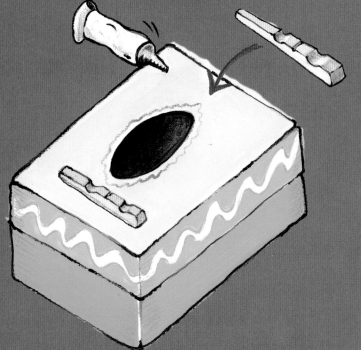

2 Tape the lid to the box. Turn the box upside down and paint it. Varnish it once the paint is dry.

3 Split the clothes peg into two halves, lengthways. Glue both halves to the box, one on either side of the hole.

Stretch the rubber bands around the box, fitting them into the grooves of the clothes pegs.

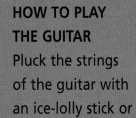

HOW TO PLAY THE GUITAR
Pluck the strings of the guitar with an ice-lolly stick or wooden spatula.

Bird caller

thin hollow cardboard, plastic or metal tube ● wooden spoon (with a handle thin enough to slide into the tube) ● twig masking tape ● gouache paints ● paintbrush PVA glue or varnish

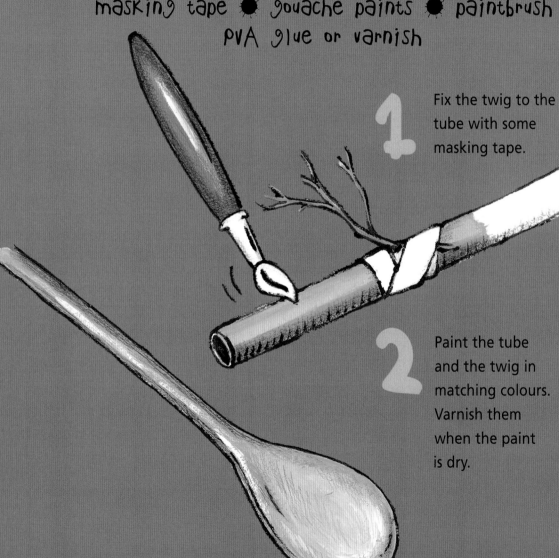

1 Fix the twig to the tube with some masking tape.

2 Paint the tube and the twig in matching colours. Varnish them when the paint is dry.

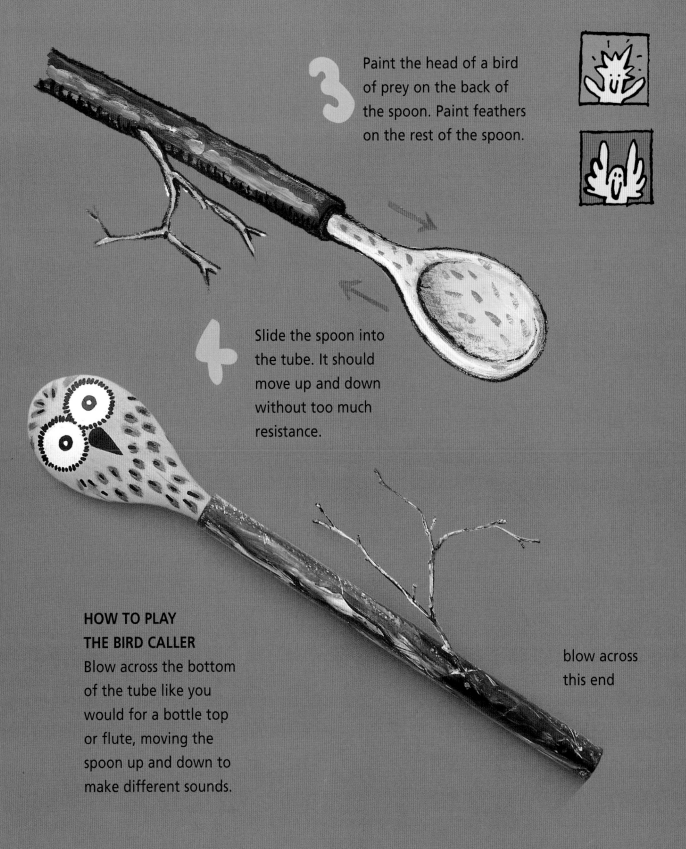

3 Paint the head of a bird of prey on the back of the spoon. Paint feathers on the rest of the spoon.

4 Slide the spoon into the tube. It should move up and down without too much resistance.

**HOW TO PLAY
THE BIRD CALLER**
Blow across the bottom of the tube like you would for a bottle top or flute, moving the spoon up and down to make different sounds.

blow across this end

Musical bugs

two smooth pebbles ● gouache paints
paintbrush ● PVA glue or varnish

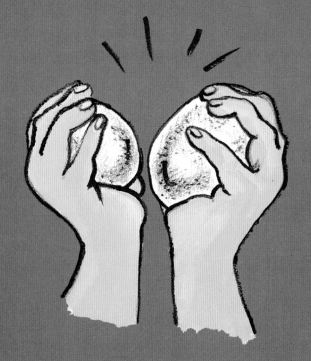

1 Find two smooth pebbles that fit snugly into your hands. Try out several kinds until you find ones that make a loud clack when you hit them together.

2 Paint the pebbles as ladybirds or other colourful bugs. When the paint is dry, add a coat of varnish.

HOW TO PLAY
MUSICAL BUGS
Knock the pebbles together in a steady, rhythmical way.

crocodile scraper

corrugated card ● pencil ● scissors ● green gouache paint
paintbrush ● PVA glue or varnish ● two marbles ● glue
plastic bottle with square, corrugated sides ● ice-lolly stick

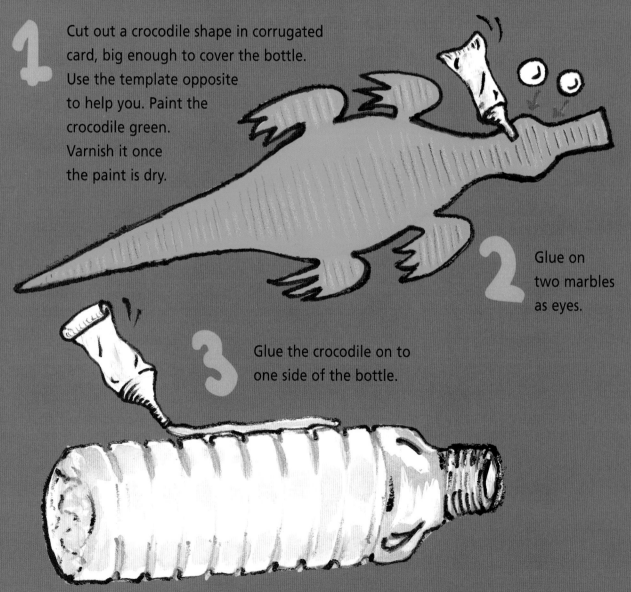

1 Cut out a crocodile shape in corrugated card, big enough to cover the bottle. Use the template opposite to help you. Paint the crocodile green. Varnish it once the paint is dry.

2 Glue on two marbles as eyes.

3 Glue the crocodile on to one side of the bottle.

28

HOW TO PLAY
THE SCRAPER

Hold the bottle in one
hand. Scrape the tip
of the lolly stick back
and forth along the
crocodile's back, making
rhythmical sounds.

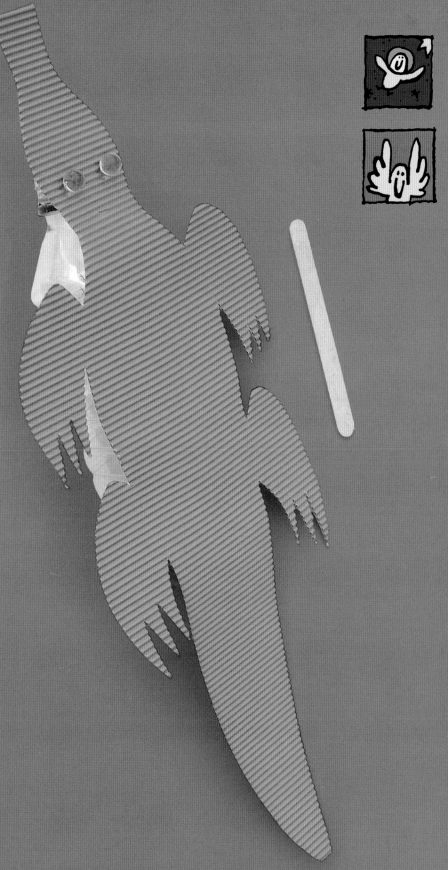

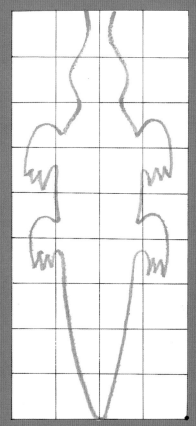

crocodile
template

Index

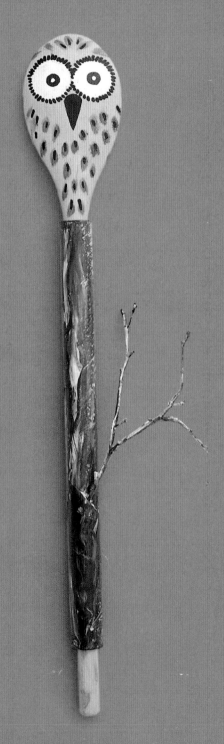